YOU CANNOT HURT ME ANYMORE

CARISSA KAUFFMAN

You Cannot Hurt Me Anymore
© 2021 Carissa Kauffman

ISBN 978-1-66780-384-5

TABLE OF CONTENTS

DENIAL

ANGER

BARGAINING

DEPRESSION

ACCEPTANCE

DENIAL

LIPS

I still don't remember all of it

Ony the way your cracked hands moved against my lips

The lips that yearned for the words to say

The lips that wanted so badly to yell "stop"

But couldn't

The lips that wished they could taste anything else

Rather than the lingering taste of the whiskey you'd drank too much of

The lips that would eventually tell every other person like you to fuck off

MY BED

Did my whole body trembling not get the point across?
The point that I didn't want your body on top of mine

I felt as if my body was shaking the entire Earth
Calling out for help to anybody that could feel it,
Or maybe even hear it

But all your body could do was shake the bed that was once mine
The bed that still holds trapped memories that I can barely distinguish
The bed that still holds your scent of worthlessness & disgust

The bed that I will eventually take back as my own

RAZOR BLADES

I hadn't craved the sharpness of a razor blade against my skin
since adolescence

My body hadn't felt this lifeless in years

My body wasn't mine anymore

My body purely belongs to the cloudy, but daunting memory of
that night

And the thought of razor blades pressed against my skin

It couldn't be nearly as painful, right?

It couldn't be nearly as sharp as the words you said

It couldn't pierce my skin as much as your drunken ego pierced
my innocence,

Right?

SHOWER

I showered seven times after you left

I didn't know what I was scrubbing off of me so viciously

Maybe the disgust that I had for myself in the moment

Maybe the uncertainty of what I'm supposed to be feeling

Maybe it was the hot water pounding against my head

In an effort to forget everything

Not just from the night it happened

But from all my life too

I didn't care at that point

Anything that would make me forget how meaningless life felt in the moment

But my head was like a sponge and only soaked the memories up

I guess I couldn't deny it anymore

SAVE ME

I wish it were easy

I wish someone could come take these feelings away

I wish someone would come purify me

Sterilize me

Sweeten me up

I wish it were that easy

ANGER

RED

I went to the water the next day

Maybe the water could tell me why the fuck I deserved that

Maybe the waves would flow so carelessly toward me

As you flowed so effortlessly into my bedroom

While your clothes were so effortlessly shedding off of your body

And I stood there in mere, frozen disbelief

I always thought this would never happen to me

Maybe is was the red bathing suit I was wearing

Red is a sinful color, right?

LISTEN

With a clenched jaw & a dry mouth
I muttered the words "get out"
That wasn't enough

Was your ego so big & manly & powerful
Maybe that toxic masculinity was too loud for you to hear my words
Was your ego fueling off of the forever damage you just bestowed
unto me?

Not until my soft, shaky voice told you to "drive safe" did you listen
Not until I shrunk myself down to fit in your back pocket did you listen
Not until I let you leave with no idea the pain you just caused me did
you listen

I hope you're listening now

IS IT OKAY?

What the fuck is wrong with you?
What made you think it was okay?

Telling me you hated me would've been okay
Telling me I was ugly would've been okay
Saying you never wanted to see me again would've been okay
What deemed your violent act against me as okay?

Was my shaking frame okay to you?
Was my hyperventilating okay to you?
Were my pain-filled, lifeless eyes okay to you?

How about my stained-glass heart?
A once beautiful, eye-catching thing that was beaming full of love
Now burst into tiny pieces too small to ever be put back together
Or to ever be whole again

Was that okay to you?

CIGARETTES

I wish I would've burnt you with the cigarettes I chain smoked after
it happened

I wish you could feel the burning embers on your skin

Each ember slowly coming together

To form a scar that will never fully go away

Much like what you did to me

A scar that never fully goes away

RAGE

I'd never been so full of rage in my life

I'd never hated something, rather someone so much

What was once a whole person

A whole person ready to fight battles for anyone that wouldn't do the same for her

A whole person showcasing her beautifully heartbreaking sleeve of emotions

Now treading through the murky waters of life

Not being able to see what's next

Only able to see the fire within her

The fire that sparks the anger

The anger for herself

For life

For him

For everyone

INNOCENCE

God, I used to have the most innocent eyes
They beamed with such light and purity
They glistened at the mere thought of life

My pupils would dilate while looking at myself in the mirror
Much like looking at someone you love

I hope they beam like that again someday
They were once so beautiful

HOMESICK

I want to be angry so bad

I want nothing more than to have the urge to seek you out

And rip you to shreds

Anger would feel more normal than whatever the fuck I'm feeling

Anger is home

And I'm feeling homesick

BARGAINING

MAYBE

Was I asking for it?

Maybe I said the wrong thing

Maybe my naturally monotone voice gave a touch too much emotion
that night

Maybe my naturally curvy body was looking a little too provocative
that night

Maybe it was that red bathing suit

Maybe it made my pale, lifeless skin glow a little too much that night

Maybe it was my fault

BAD

What if you're not a bad person

What if you didn't mean to do what you did

What if it was an accident

What if that whiskey hit you the wrong way that night?

What if you didn't mean to hurt me?

What if you did see the beauty within me?

Possibly acted on it in the wrong way

What if you're not too bad after all?

AT HOME

I should've just gone home that night
If I would've stayed in what was once my safe space

I wouldn't have to go through months of trauma therapy
I wouldn't have to stare at my body every night
A constant battle to convince myself that this body is mine once again

Maybe if I would've just stayed the fuck at home

I would be whole again

NO MEANS NO

If I said "no" a sixth time

Maybe he wouldn't have done it

If I shouted "no" instead of softly saying it

Maybe he wouldn't have done it

If I wouldn't have froze up

If I wouldn't have just laid there,

Not a single thought in my head

Maybe he wouldn't have done it

If I would've punched him so hard,

That his football-stadium sized ego would've flew out the window

Maybe he wouldn't have done it

AS A CHILD

It is so hard

Embodying it

That something so cruel happened to me so young,

So childlike

Twice I let this happen to me

How could I?

DEPRESSION

THE VOID

Everyone's heard of rose colored glasses
Looking at life with such love & joy

But has anyone talked about murky grey-colored glasses
And on the bad days,
Black-colored glasses
Viewing life as this never-ending void
Filled to the brim with pain & misery
The void walled up with worthlessness

Maybe at the bottom there's happiness
Maybe if I dive head-first into the abyss of the unknown
I'll find what I'm looking for

I'm not strong enough to look, yet

HOUSE PLANT

I am merely a house plant
A living being constantly forgetting to be watered
Forgetting to be taken care of

The sad thing is, though
I am the one forgetting to water myself
I am the one forgetting to take care of myself
I am the one forgetting to speak kind words to myself
Words to grow & flourish again

They say if you speak negatively to a house plant
Their growth will become stagnant
Leaf by leaf the plant starts to wilt

The kind words won't come out, though
I don't know how to grow again

CAN THIS FEELING JUST GO AWAY, PLEASE?

I'm staring at the beautiful, bright blue sky

Filled with clouds shaped as butterflies, smiley faces

Even some whole hearts, too

Showing no sign of ever being broken

And it's staring back at me, too

Except the clouds are slowly morphing into his face

Cloud by cloud framing the feeling that I thought I'd gotten rid of

But slowly it sinks back in

Why can't I get away from you?

I sneak away into pure solitude,

But you always find a way to follow

MY CUP

I keep asking myself…

Is the cup half empty, or half full?

The thing is,

My cup is completely empty

Drained of anything that once filled it up

I keep trying to fill it,

But my efforts are growing shy

It's like there's a hole at the bottom of the cup

Slowly draining me

Slowly draining my spirit

Slowly letting even the most beautiful parts of my life slip through
my fingers

As I desperately try to catch the it while it's draining out of the bottom

I guess that's what depression is

A hole so deep within you

You can't ever fill it back up

YOUR GHOST

The ghost of you still lives in my home

Your voice seeping into my head every night

Reminding me of the irreversible damage that belongs within me

I still see you out of the corner of my eye

Doing a double take to make sure you're not actually there

IT IS NOT MY FAULT

I chant it around the house when I feel your presence

I didn't know you didn't have to be dead to haunt someone

FOREVER

You know what they always say
Moments end, but memories last forever

And after a year of burying them down so far I thought I'd forget
they existed
They came back to haunt me
And it's true

Whether good, or bad
Memories last forever

HYPERSEXUAL

Every man has your eyes

I don't mean for them to,

But they do

That's all I see

Shouldn't I be tapping into the sweet, sultry moments

The ones supposedly comprised of pure intimacy

Shouldn't I be focused on the lustful looks I'm given

I wish to see purely with my eyes

And not my trauma-filled brain

I wish to be able to take in these intimate moments with purity

I wish to breathe them in deeply

And for the romantic moments to seep into my lungs and never escape

I wish to take them for what they really are

Instead of the feeling of being used coursing through my veins

I'm addicted to it now, I think

Their beady, little eyes

Just like yours

Gazing at my body

Trying to decide which part of my body they want to use tonight

I wish you weren't every man I've ever met

ACCEPTANCE

YOUR TINTED WINDOWS

As I sit on my porch watching the cars drive by
Ever so fearful that I may see yours cruise by
And the possibility that we may lock eyes through your tinted windows
I think to myself

That's it
That's all that would happen

You cannot hurt me anymore
And neither can the thought of you

Because what was done can never be reversed
But, I can promise you one thing
It will never, ever be done again

And you cannot hurt me anymore

THE LAST CIGARETTE

In that pack of cigarettes I chain smoked after it happened

I always kept the last one left in the pack

And as I lit that last cigarette,

I was free

Free from the ties you put between us

Because as I exhaled that sweet, sweet smoke

Every last thought of you went with it

Every haunted memory slowly drifted into the air

Puff by puff

Breath by breath

You were gone

MY OLD BED SHEETS

I burned the old sheets on my bed
The sheets that your wretched body once made contact with
The sheets that housed your disgusting scent,
No matter how many times I washed them
The sheets that had my shaking, frozen body on them

They are merely ashes now

And as the flames went up,
So did I
Practically levitating in the fact that you were gone

Every last piece of you,
It was gone
And it was done

DEAD TO ME

Sometimes I think to myself

Your spirit is alive & well

Still out there living life with no remorse

In my eyes, though

You're dead to me

Through all of the laughs,

The good times,

The memories

You knew exactly how you were going to hurt me

And I used to blame myself for being so blind to it

But,

I was never looking for deceitfulness & evil when I looked into your eyes

When I tried to learn what your soul was comprised of,

I was never looking for hate, or bad intentions

I could never really grasp onto anything, though

Because you never had one

Now I know

FINALLY

I've found myself again

I keep finding out new things about myself everyday

Finding out what new me likes

Discovering the ways to make new me feel safe

Tuning into the new emotions I have

It's the hardest thing I've ever done

But my God, is it worth it

I finally want to live again

MY REFLECTION

And as I sit in the mirror
Staring at myself with what used to be shame & disgust
Now has turned into badassery & strength

My reflection doesn't tell me I'm worthless anymore
It shouts that I didn't deserve what happened to me
It shouts that I should be proud of myself for sticking around,
Even if just a few months ago,
I was convinced that it was my time to go

My reflection now stares back at me with unconditional love

It tells me to look at myself with the soft, loving eyes
That I once looked at everyone with

It tells me that somehow,
In some way,

Everything is gonna be okay

R.I.P

Grief stricken is a way to describe it

Losing a piece of yourself

One that you'd thought would live forever

Grief is just an absence

And grieving yourself is sometimes much harder than grieving a loved one

When a loved one passes on

The heavy grief is momentarily filled

With flowers, family, & memories

When you lose a piece of yourself

It stays empty awhile

Because I definitely don't want memories to fill the empty space

No one gives you flowers, or cooks you a meal after you get assaulted

Shit, some people won't even believe it

And that's the harsh, but true reality of it all

But in the midst of all the emotional turmoil

Just know that there are so many people who love & support you

Even in this fucked up society

You are never alone

TOO MUCH, TOO SOON, TOO FAST

As I sit & think about everything that happened

It wa all too much,

Too soon,

Too fast

Barely able to comprehend it until months passed on

I thought to myself

How can I ever be normal again?

But the truth is,

Normal is purely a facade

Normal is never the same

It is always effortlessly changing

But the beautiful part of it all is,

Even when you're surrounded by horror & pain

Eventually, you will come back to yourself

You will be "normal" again

While normal used to look like a meadow field of flowers with bright
blue skies,

Normal is now a rainstorm with bright lighting strikes & loud thunder

They are two very different things,

But still hold just as much beauty as the other

Although, some days will be harder than others
Throughout it all,
If I could ask one thing
Please choose not to live your life in pain

Do not continue to seek your old "normals"
Because they do not resonate anymore

Look for new "normals"
The ones that make your soul light up with passion,
And the ones that make your eyes beam with life just a little brighter

Because that is who you are now,
A beautiful being
Searching for new things to bring love into your life
Things that surround your life with bright, white light

You can do it
I believe in you,
I love you,
& I will always stand with you